To: Geraldine

From: Liz

THE JOYS OF
CHRISTMAS

THE JOYS OF CHRISTMAS

NELSON R. WILSON

WILLIAM MORROW AND COMPANY, INC.
NEW YORK

CONTENTS

THE JOYS OF
CHRISTMAS

I

'TIS THE SEASON

Deck the hall with boughs of holly,
'Tis the season to be jolly,
Don we now our gay apparel,
Troll the ancient Christmas carol
Fa-la-la-la-la la-la-la-la

hristmas, children, is not a date. It is
a state of mind.

MARY ELLEN CHASE

It is impossible to conceive of any holiday that
could take its place, nor indeed would it seem that
human wit could invent another so adapted to
humanity.

CHARLES DUDLEY WARNER

The merry Christmas, with its generous boards,
Its fire-lit hearths, and gifts and blazing trees,
Its pleasant voices uttering gentle words,
Its genial mirth, attuned to sweet accords,
Its holiest memories!
The fairest season of the passing year—
The merry, merry Christmas time is here.

GEORGE ARNOLD

Blessed is the season which engages the whole world
in a conspiracy of love.

HAMILTON WRIGHT MABIE

13

Happy, happy Christmas, that can win us back
to the delusions of our childhood days, recall to the
old man the pleasures of his youth, and transport
the traveler back to his own fireside and quiet
home!

CHARLES DICKENS

England was merry England, when
Old Christmas brought his sports again.
'Twas Christmas broach'd the mightiest ale;
'Twas Christmas told the merriest tale;
A Christmas gambol oft could cheer
The poor man's heart through half the year.

SIR WALTER SCOTT

What though upon his hoary head
Have fallen many a winter's snow?
His wreath is still as green and red
As 'twas a thousand years ago.
For what has he to do with care!
His wassail-bowl and old arm-chair
Are ever standing ready there,
For Christmas comes but once a year.

THOMAS MILLER

Christmas is here,
Merry old Christmas,
Gift-bearing, heart-touching,
Joy-bringing Christmas,
Day of grand memories,
King of the year!

WASHINGTON IRVING

Dearer than memory, brighter than
expectation is the ever returning *now* of Christmas.
Why else, each time we greet its return, should
happiness ring out in us like a peal of bells?

ELIZABETH BOWEN

nd well our Christmas sires of old
Loved when the year its course had rolled
And brought blithe Christmas back again,
With all his hospitable train.

SIR WALTER SCOTT

Christmas comes! He comes, he comes,
Ushered with a rain of plums;
Hollies in the window greet him;
Schools come driving post to meet him;
Gifts precede him, bells proclaim him,
Every mouth delights to name him. . . .

LEIGH HUNT

Holly and Holiness
Come well together,
Christ-Child and Santa Claus
Share the white weather;
Plums in plum pudding and
Turkey with dressing,
Choirs singing Carols—
All have his blessing.

RALPH W. SEAGER

There was always a church play on Christmas
Eve, given at great cost to bed sheets and tempers. I
was usually an anonymous shepherd with
instructions to keep my grating voice low so as not
to interfere with those who could sing. However,
the shepherds carried crooks, which we used with
deadly effect to trip the ankles of the splendid
characters who had been the saintly Joseph and the
Wise Men a few minutes before. The star that led
the wise men across the desert traveled on a wire
across the tiny stage, and often stuck halfway
across, long before it reached the corner which was
the barn where Joseph and Mary and the Child lay.
One of the shepherds would then lift his crook to
the starry heavens and shove that wayward star over
where it belonged, sometimes bringing down the
skies themselves.

PAUL ENGLE

Last year I participated in the lighting of the tree in Rockefeller Center. There were people everywhere—dignified big shots, tired-out office workers, rushing shoppers—all faiths, no faiths, all sizes and colors. And then somebody pressed the button and the tree sprang to life and the music burst forth and the glory in the air was unmistakable. People were transformed! They had been mystically changed by this thing called Christmas!

NORMAN VINCENT PEALE

Blessed by Christmas sunshine, our natures, perhaps long leafless, bring forth new love, new kindness, new mercy, new compassion.

HELEN KELLER

The earth has grown old with its burden of care
    But at Christmas it is always young,
The heart of the jewel burns lustrous and fair
And its soul full of music breaks forth on the air,
    When the song of the angels is sung.

PHILLIPS BROOKS

It is a beautiful arrangement, also, derived from days of yore, that this festival, which commemorates the announcement of the religion of peace and love, has been made the season for gathering together of family connections, and drawing closer again those bands of kindred hearts, which the cares and pleasures and sorrows of the world are continually operating to cast loose: of calling back the children of a family, who have launched forth in life, and wandered widely assunder, once more to assemble about the paternal hearth, that rallying place of the affections, there to grow young and loving again among the endearing mementos of childhood.

WASHINGTON IRVING

I wish you all a special Christmas this year, preferably with a lovely tree, hung with ornaments from your childhood. (A battered pinwheel still hangs on ours, left from my baby days. It was kept at my grandmother's house, and has fallen into my hands now—and still delights my children.) I wish you a fat turkey, or a goose . . . Christmas cookies . . . Christmas songs, but *most* important, people you love to share it.

DANIELLE STEEL

Will you please stop pulling at me. I did buy
my Christmas cards last January. I just can't find
them.

ERMA BOMBECK

Mother didn't expect to have anything to do
with the Christmas pageant except to make me and
my little brother, Charlie, be in it (we didn't want
to) and to make my father go and see it (he didn't
want to).

Every year he said the same thing—"I've seen
the Christmas pageant."

"You haven't seen this year's Christmas
pageant," Mother would tell him. "Charlie's a
shepherd this year."

"Charlie was a shepherd last year. No . . . you
go on and go. I'm just going to put on my bathrobe
and sit by the fire and relax. There's never anything
different about the Christmas pageant."

"There's something different this year,"
Mother said.

"What?"

"Charlie is wearing your bathrobe."

So that year my father went to the Christmas
pageant . . . to see his bathrobe, he said.

BARBARA ROBINSON

When it comes to Christmas, there are two
kinds of people, orderly and disorderly. Orderly
people have all their Christmas cards mailed by
December tenth. Disorderly people say, "December
tenth! Good Grief, I thought it was *November*
tenth."

WILL STANTON

Christmas is when your mailbox is so full that
it doesn't echo.

"CHARLIE BROWN,"
alias Charles M. Schulz.

The log was in the fireplace
    all spiced and set to burn.
At last the yearly Christmas race
    was in the clubhouse turn.
The cards were in the mail
    all the gifts beneath the tree,
And thirty days' reprieve
    till VISA could catch up with me.

TOM HEGG

There's nothing like an old-fashioned Christmas—goodies on the groaning board, halls decked with holly berry, gaily wrapped presents piling up on the window sills, loved ones chiming carols. It can put you flat on your back for a month.

JEAN KERR

I am the joy of Christmas. Try revealing that to a temporary salesperson at Bloomingdale's around the fifteenth of December. If only, when I hand them my credit card, they wouldn't grin idiotically and say, "Oh, well, for you it's Christmas every day, isn't it?" Ho, ho, ho, even so.

JOYCE S. CHRISTMAS

That clicking sound you hear about this time is the result of fourteen million husbands pushing the panic button. They are pushing it because they are hours away from Christmas and still have no gift for what's-her-name, mother of his four children.

ERMA BOMBECK

Good King Wenceslas looked out,
On the feast of Stephen,
When the snow lay round about,
Deep and crisp and even:
Brightly shone the moon that night,
Though the frost was cruel,
When a poor man came in sight,
Gath'ring winter fuel.

"Hither, page, and stand by me,
If thou know'st it, telling,
Yonder peasant, who is he?
Where and what his dwelling?"
"Sire, he lives a good league hence,
Underneath the mountain,
Right against the forest fence,
By Saint Agnes' fountain."

"Bring me flesh, and bring me wine,
Bring me pine-logs hither:
Thou and I will see him dine,
When we bear them thither."
Page and monarch, forth they went,
Forth they went together;
Through the rude wind's wild lament
And the bitter weather.

"Sire, the night is darker now,
And the wind grows stronger;
Fails my heart, I know not how;
I can go no longer."
"Mark my footsteps, my good page;
Tread thou in them boldly:
Thou shalt find the winter's rage
Freeze thy blood less coldly."

In his master's steps he trod,
Where the snow lay dinted.
Heat was in the very sod
Which the saint had printed.
Therefore, Christian men, be sure,
Wealth or rank possessing,
Ye who now will bless the poor,
Shall yourselves find blessing.

JOHN MASON NEALE

Love came down at Christmas,
    Love all lovely, Love Divine;
Love was born at Christmas,
    Stars and Angels gave the sign.

CHRISTINA ROSSETTI

"I have often thought," says Sir Roger, "it happens very well that Christmas should fall in the middle of the winter. It is the most dead, uncomfortable time of the year, when the poor people would suffer very much from their poverty and cold, if they had not good cheer, warm fires, and Christmas gambols to support them."

JOSEPH ADDISON

May you
have the gladness
of Christmas
which is hope;
The spirit
of Christmas
Which is peace;
The heart
of Christmas
Which is love.

ADA V. HENDRICKS

Christmas
is coming,
the geese are
getting fat,
Won't you please
put a penny
in a poor man's hat?
If you haven't
got a penny
a ha'penny will do.
If you haven't
got a ha'penny,
Then God bless you!

ANONYMOUS

Last year I read Charles Dickens' *A Christmas Carol* and couldn't get over how good it was. I guess everyone else knew but me.

ANDY ROONEY

Good luck unto old Christmas
    And long life let us sing.
For he doth more good unto the poor
    Than many a crownèd king!

MARY HOWITT

Snow lay on the croft and river-bank in
undulations softer than the limbs of infancy; it lay
with the neatliest finished border of every sloping
roof, making the dark red gables stand out with a
new depth of colour; it weighed heavily on the
laurels and fir-trees, till it fell from them with a
shuddering sound . . . there was no gleam, no
shadow, for the heavens, too, were one still, pale
cloud—no sound or motion in anything but the
dark river that flowed and moaned like an unresting
sorrow. But old Christmas smiled as he laid this
cruel-seeming spell on the out-door world, for he
meant to light up home with a new brightness, to
deepen all the richness of in-door colour, and give a
keener edge of delight to warm fragrance of food;
he meant to prepare a sweet imprisonment that
would strengthen the primitive fellowship of
kindred, and make the sunshine of familiar human
faces as welcome as the hidden day-star.

GEORGE ELIOT

. . . The bells ceased as they had begun, together. They were succeeded by a clanking noise, deep down below, as if some person were dragging a heavy chain over the casks in the wine-merchant's cellar. Scrooge then remembered to have heard that ghosts in haunted houses were described as dragging chains.

The cellar door flew open with a booming sound, and then he heard the noise much louder, on the floors below; then coming up the stairs; then coming straight towards his door.

"It's humbug still!" said Scrooge. "I won't believe it."

His colour changed, though, when, without a pause, it came on through the heavy door, and passed into the room before his eyes. Upon its coming in, the dying flame leaped up, as though it cried, "I know him! Marley's ghost!" and fell again.

CHARLES DICKENS

And he who gives a child a treat
Makes joy-bells ring in Heaven's street.
And he who gives a child a home
Builds palaces in Kingdom Come.
And she who gives a baby birth,
Brings Saviour Christ again to earth.
For life is joy and mind is fruit,
And body's precious earth and root.

JOHN MASEFIELD

Let the children have their night of fun and laughter, let the gifts of Father Christmas delight their play. Let us grown-ups share to the full in their unstinted pleasures before we turn again to the stern tasks and formidable years that lie before us, resolved that by our sacrifice and daring these same children shall not be robbed of their inheritance or denied their right to live in a free and decent world.

And so, in God's mercy, a happy Christmas to you all.

WINSTON CHURCHILL
in a Christmas Eve speech from
the White House during a visit
to America in 1941.

Personally i do not care a d. whether Marley was dead or not it is just that there is something about the xmas Carol which makes paters and grown ups read with grate XPRESION, and this is very embarrassing for all. It is all right for the first part they just roll the r's a lot but wate till they come to scrooge's newphew. When he sa Mery Christmas uncle it is like a H-bomb explosion and so it goes on until you get to Tiny Tim chiz chiz chiz he is a weed. When Tiny Tim sa God bless us every one your pater is so overcome he burst out blubbering. By this time boys have bitten through their ropes and make good their escape so 9000000000 boos to bob crachit.

GEOFFREY WILLIAMS

27

Loving Father, help us remember the birth of Jesus, that we may share in the song of the angels, the gladness of the shepherds, and the worship of the wise men.

Close the door of hate and open the door of love all over the world.

Let kindness come with every gift and good desires with every greeting.

Deliver us from evil by the blessing which Christ brings, and teach us to be merry with clear hearts.

May the Christmas morning make us happy to be thy children, and the Christmas evening bring us to our beds with grateful thoughts, forgiving and forgiven, for Jesus' sake. Amen!

ROBERT LOUIS STEVENSON

So remember while December
Brings the Christmas day,
In the year let there be Christmas
In the things you do and say;
Wouldn't life be worth the living
Wouldn't dreams be coming true
If we kept the Christmas spirit
All the whole year through?

ANONYMOUS

"I don't know what day of the month it is," said Scrooge. "I don't know how long I have been among the Spirits. I don't know anything. I'm quite a baby. Never mind; I don't care. I'd rather be a baby. Hallo! Whoop! Hallo here!"

He was checked in his transports by the churches ringing out the lustiest peals he had ever heard. Clash, clash, hammer; ding, dong, bell. Bell, dong, ding; hammer, clang, clash! Oh, glorious, glorious!

Running to the window, he opened it, and put his head out. No fog, no mist; clear, bright, jovial, stirring, cold; cold piping for the blood to dance to; golden sunlight; Heavenly sky; sweet fresh air; merry bells. Oh, glorious, glorious!

"What's today?" cried Scrooge, calling downward to a boy in Sunday clothes, who perhaps had loitered in to look about him.

"Eh?" returned the boy, with all his might of wonder.

"What's today, my fine fellow?" said Scrooge.

"Today!" replied the boy. "Why, CHRISTMAS DAY."

CHARLES DICKENS

Back over the black mystery of old years, forward into the black mystery of the years to come, shines ever more confident the golden kindliness of Christmas.

WINIFRED KIRKLAND

At Christmas I no more desire a rose
Than wish a snow in May's new-fangled
  mirth;
But like of each thing that in season
  grows.

WILLIAM SHAKESPEARE

 like days
  when feathers are snowing,
  and all the caves
  have petticoats showing,
  and the air is cold,
  and the wires are humming,
  but you feel all warm . . .
  with Christmas coming!

AILEEN FISHER

Oh, give me an old-fashioned Christmas card,
With hostlers hostling in an old inn yard,
With church bells chiming their silver notes,
And jolly red squires in their jolly red coats,
And a good fat goose by the fire that dangles,
And a few more angels and a few less angles.
Turn backward, Time, to please this bard,
And give me an old-fashioned Christmas card.

OGDEN NASH

Some say that ever 'gainst that season comes
Wherein our Saviour's birth is celebrated
The bird of dawning singeth all night long;
And then, they say, no spirit dare stir abroad,
The nights are wholesome, then no planets strike,
No fairy takes, nor witch hath power to charm,
So hallow'd and so gracious is the time.

WILLIAM SHAKESPEARE

The next morning was one of those miraculous sunrises that occur now and then in a lifetime, but only in the country. The night had been damp and still and cold, and by morning every branch and twig of tree and bush was coated with thick jagged frost crystals. The sunrise was of the flaming red variety that constitutes a warning to fishermen and shepherds in the old saying. For a little while it touched each frost crystal and turned it pink. Everything we could see, hills, pastures, trees, fences—was a frosty, sparkling pink. I had once seen a pink snowstorm, a heavy but limited fall of snow over a valley with the rays of the setting sun shining through it. That was lovely, but this was miraculous, for it transformed everything we could see into a rosy fairyland on Christmas Day in the morning.

GLADYS OGDEN DIMOCK

Now Christmas is come,
Let's beat up the drum,
And call all our neighbors together,
And when they appear,
Let us make them such cheer
As will keep out the wind and the weather.

WASHINGTON IRVING

"Well, Mr. Arbuthnot, I'm a thousand times
obliged to you. I didn't realize there were so many
Christmas clichés."

"Son, Christmas is full of them—good,
wholesome, warming clichés that soften, if only for
a few days, the bitterness and heartache that fill the
world. Clichés about holly and mistletoe and Yule
logs and wassail, and Tiny Tims and Scrooges,
about people thinking about other people for a
change, about Christmas vacations and families
reunited, about churchgoers leaving midnight Mass
and calling cheery greetings to one another as they
hurry home through the friendly snow to trim the
trees, about goodwill to men—yes, and about peace
on earth and the hope of it. My boy, 'Merry
Christmas' is the noblest and kindliest cliché that
ever was, and if the day should come when men will
no longer have the heart to wish their neighbors a
Merry Christmas and a Happy New Year, on that
day the human race will have real reason to
despair."

FRANK SULLIVAN

32

Whosoever on ye nighte of ye nativity of ye young Lord Jesus, in ye great snows, shall fare forth bearing a succulent bone for ye loste and lamenting hounde, a whisp of hay for ye shivering horse, a cloak of warm raiment for ye stranded wayfarer, a bundle of faggots for ye twittering crone, a flagon of red wine for him whose marrow withers, a garland of bright berries for one who has worn chains, gay arias of lute and harp for all huddled birds who thought that song was dead, and delivers lush sweetmeats for such babes' faces as peer from lonely windows—

To him shall be proffered and returned gifts of such an astonishment as will rival the hues of the peacock and the harmonies of heavens so that though he live to ye great age when man goes stopping and querulous because of the nothing that is left in him, yet shall he walk upright and remembering, as one whose heart shines like a great star in his breast.

Anonymous

If any of you have any quarrels, or misunderstandings, or coolnesses, or cold shoulders, or shynesses, or tiffs, or miffs, or huffs, with any one else, just make friends before Christmas,—you will be so much merrier if you do.

I ask it of you for the sake of that old angelic song, heard so many years ago by the shepherds, keeping watch by night, on Bethlehem Heights.

Charles Dickens

Ah, friends, dear friends, as years go on
    and heads get gray, how fast the
    guests do go!
Touch hands, touch hands, with those
    that stay.
Strong hands to weak, old hands to
    young, around the Christmas
    board, touch hands.
The false forget, the foe forgive, for
    every guest will go and every fire
    burn low and cabin empty stand.
Forget, forgive, for who may say that
    Christmas day may ever come to
    host or guest again.
Touch hands!

WILLIAM HENRY HARRISON MURRAY

Christmas is not all color and music, bells
and candles, and gifts. It's not all tradition and
memories and the delight of introducing very young
people to something glittering and lovely and new
to them. It is also a moment of quiet meditation, of
remembering in a very personal way those who will
not stand again at the door, laughing, or sit with us
at the table.

FAITH BALDWIN

"Dickens is dead." Beneath that grievous cry
London seemed shivering in the summer heat:
Strangers took up the tale like friends that meet:
"Dickens is dead," said they, and hurried by;
Street children stopped their games—they knew
    not why,
But some new night seemed darkening down the
    street;
A girl in rags, staying her way-worn feet,
Cried, "Dickens is dead? Will Father Christmas
    die?"
City he loved, take courage on thy way,
He loves thee still in all thy joys and fears:
Though he whose smiles made bright thine eyes of
    gray—
Whose brave sweet voice, uttering thy tongueless
    years,
Made laughters bubble through thy sea of tears—
Is gone, Dickens returns on Christmas day.

THEODORE WATTS

"God bless us every one!" said Tiny Tim, the
last of all.

CHARLES DICKENS

II

JOY TO THE WORLD

Joy to the world! the Lord is come;
Let earth receive her King;
Let every heart prepare Him room,
And heaven and nature sing,
And heaven and nature sing.

The Son shall lead the life
   of Gods, and be
By Gods and Heroes seen, and Gods
   and Heroes see.
The jarring Nations he in peace shall bind,
And with paternal Virtues rule Mankind.
Unbidden Earth shall wreathing Ivy bring
And fragrant Herbs (the promises of Spring)
As her first offerings to her infant King.

VIRGIL
*These lines were written nearly
half a century before the
birth of Christ.*

Light looked down and beheld Darkness.
   "Thither will I go," said Light.
Peace looked down and beheld War.
   "Thither will I go," said Peace.
Love looked down and beheld Hatred.
   "Thither will I go," said Love.
So came Light, and shone.
So came Peace, and gave rest.
So came Love, and brought life.
And the word was made Flesh,
   and dwelt among us.

LAURENCE HOUSEMAN

The first Nowell the angel did say,
Was to certain poor shepherds in fields as they lay;
In fields where they lay, keeping their sheep,
In a cold winter's night that was so deep:

Nowell, Nowell, Nowell, Nowell,
Born is the King of Israel.

They looked up and saw a star,
Shining in the east, beyond them far;
And to the earth it gave great light,
And so it continued both day and night:

Nowell, Nowell, Nowell, Nowell,
Born is the King of Israel.

TRADITIONAL CAROL

It came upon the midnight clear
    That glorious song of old
From angels bending near the earth
    To touch their harps of gold;
"Peace on the earth, good will to men
    From Heaven's all-gracious King"—
The world in solemn stillness lay
    To hear the angels sing.

EDMUND HAMILTON SEARS

    This is Christmas Day, the anniversary of the
world's greatest event. To one day all the early
world looked forward; to the same day, the latter
world looks back. That day holds time together.

ALEXANDER SMITH

And there were in the same country shepherds abiding in the field, keeping watch over their flock by night.

And, lo, the angel of the Lord came upon them, and the glory of the Lord shone round about them; and they were sore afraid.

And the angel said unto them, Fear not: for behold, I bring you good tidings of great joy, which shall be to all people.

For unto you is born this day, in the city of David, a Saviour, which is Christ the Lord.

And this shall be a sign unto you; Ye shall find the babe wrapped in swaddling clothes, lying in a manger.

And suddenly there was with the angel a multitude of the heavenly host praising God, and saying,

Glory to God in the highest, and on earth peace, good will toward men.

And it came to pass, as the angels were gone away from them into heaven, the shepherds said one to another, Let us now go even unto Bethlehem, and see this thing which is come to pass, which the Lord hath made known unto us.

And they came with haste, and found Mary and Joseph, and the babe lying in a manger.

SAINT LUKE

Good news from heaven the angels bring
Glad tidings to the earth they sing:
To us this day a child is given,
To crown us with the joy of heaven.

MARTIN LUTHER

We saw a light shine out a-far,
On Christmas in the morning.
Then did we fall on bend-ed knee,
On Christmas in the morning,
And praised the Lord, who'd let us
See His glory at its dawning.

MEDIEVAL ENGLISH CAROL

Welcome, all wonders in one sight!
Eternity shut in a span!
Summer in winter, day in night!
Heaven in earth, and God in man!
Great little One! whose all-embracing birth
Lifts earth to heaven, stoops heaven to earth!

RICHARD CRASHAW

Go tell it on the mountain,
Over the hills and everywhere;
Go tell it on the mountain,
That Jesus Christ is born.

OLD SPIRITUAL

See amid the winter's snow,
Born for us on earth below;
See the tender Lamb appears,
Promised from eternal years:
Hail thou ever-blessed morn;
Hail redemption's happy dawn;
Sing through all Jerusalem,
Christ is born in Bethlehem.

E. CASWALL

Shepherds, rejoice, lift up your eyes,
    And send your fears away;
News from the region of the skies!
    Salvation's born today.

ISAAC WATTS

Oh, see the air is shaken with white and
    heavenly wings—
This is the Lord of all the earth, this is the
    King of Kings.

RICHARD WATSON GILDER

I sing the birth was born tonight,
The author both of earth and light;
    The angels so did sound it,
And, like the ravished shepherds said,
Who saw the light, and were afraid,
    Yet searched, and true they found it.

BEN JONSON

43

Oh, the little stars sang down to Him
And the moon she gave a crown to Him
And the snow a silver carpet for His throne
And the oxen by the manger
Did homage to the Stranger. . . .

CHARLES WILLIAM STUBBS

Christmas Eve, and twelve of the clock.
"Now they are all on their knees,"
An elder said as we sat in a flock
By the embers in hearthside ease.

We pictured the meek mild creatures where
They dwelt in their strawy pen,
Nor did it occur to one of us there
To doubt they were kneeling then.

So fair a fancy few would weave
In these years! Yet, I feel,
If someone said on Christmas Eve,
"Come; see the oxen kneel,

"In the lonely barton by yonder coomb
Our childhood used to know,"
I should go with him in the gloom,
Hoping it might be so.

THOMAS HARDY

Hay! hay did you say?
Surely it was not hay
On which the Christ-Child lay?
Humble indeed the shed,
Awkward the manger bed,
Was there no linen spread?
Come, was it hay you said?

Yes, it was common hay,
Cut on a summer's day.
As the sweet crop they drest—
Dividing good from best—
They knew not some would rest
The world's most holy Guest.

ANONYMOUS

O come, little children, O come one and all!
O come to the cradle in Bethlehem's stall!
Come, look in the manger! There sleeps on the hay
An infant so lovely, in light bright as day.

CHRISTOPH VON SCHMID

Oh, ye shepherds,
Gaze in awe,
On a sight
No eyes yet saw!
Christ sleeps in
A stable's gloom
Come to save us
From our doom.

YUGOSLAVIAN CAROL

A little child,
   A shining star.
A stable rude,
   The door ajar.

Yet in that place,
   So crude, forlorn,
The Hope of all
   The world was born.

ANONYMOUS

Before the paling of the stars,
   Before the winter morn,
   Before the earliest cockcrow
Jesus Christ was born:
    Born in a stable,
   Cradled in a manger,
In the world His hands had made
   Born a stranger.

CHRISTINA ROSSETTI

Away in a manger, no crib for a bed,
The little Lord Jesus laid down His sweet head.
The stars in the bright sky looked down
   where He lay—
The little Lord Jesus asleep on the hay.

The cattle are lowing, the baby awakes,
But little Lord Jesus no crying He makes.
I love Thee, Lord Jesus, look down from the sky,
And stay by my side till the morning is nigh.

MARTIN LUTHER

46

There are some of us . . . who think to
ourselves, "If I had only been there! How quick I
would have been to help the Baby. I would have
washed His linen. How happy I would have been to
go with the shepherds to see the Lord lying in the
manger! Yes, we would. We say that because we
know how great Christ is, but if we had been there
at that time, we would have done no better than
the people of Bethlehem. . . . Why don't we do it
now? We have Christ in our neighbor.

MARTIN LUTHER

Little Jesus, wast Thou shy
Once, and just so small as I?
And what did it feel like to be
Out of Heaven, and just like me?
Didst thou sometimes think of *there*
And ask where all the angels were?
I should think that I would cry
For my house made all of sky;
I would look about the air,
And wonder where my angels were;
And at waking 'twould distress me—
Not an angel there to dress me!

FRANCIS THOMPSON

At Christmas, Christ comes to us like a little child, small and helpless, so much in need of all that love can give. Are we ready to receive Him? Before the birth of Jesus His parents asked for a simple dwelling place, but there was none. If Mary and Joseph were looking for a home for Jesus, would they choose your house and all it holds?

MOTHER TERESA

Could I know
That they were so important? Just the two,
No servants, just a workman sort of man,
Leading a donkey, and his wife thereon
Drooping and pale—I saw them not myself,
My servants must have driven them away;
But had I seen them—how was I to know?
Were inns to welcome stragglers up and down
In all our towns from Beersheba to Dan,
Till He should come? And how were men to know?

AMOS RUSSEL WELLS

O, to have dwelt in Bethlehem
    When the star of the Lord shone bright!
To have sheltered the holy wanderers
    On that blessed Christmas night;
To have kissed the tender wayworn feet
    Of the Mother undefiled,
And, with reverent wonder and deep delight,
    To have tended the Holy Child!

ADELAIDE A. PROCTOR

O Little town of Bethlehem,
How still we see thee lie!
Above thy deep and dreamless sleep
The silent stars go by.
Yet in thy dark streets shineth
The everlasting light;
The hopes and fears of all the years
Are met in thee tonight.

Phillips Brooks

Silent night, holy night!
All is calm, all is bright,
Round yon Virgin Mother and Child,
Holy Infant so tender and mild,
Sleep in heavenly peace,
Sleep in heavenly peace.

Joseph Mohr

See the kinder shepherds round Him
    Telling wonders from the sky!
Where they sought Him, there they found Him,
    With His Virgin mother by.

Isaac Watts

Rise, happy morn; rise holy morn;
    Draw forth the cheerful day from night;
    O Father, touch the east and light
The light that shone when hope was born.

Alfred, Lord Tennyson

f the three Wise Men
Who came to the King
One was a brown man,
So they sing.

Of the three Wise Men
Who followed the Star
One was a brown king
From afar. . . .

Unto His humble
Manger they came
And bowed their heads
In Jesus' name.

Three wise Men,
One dark like me—
Part of His
Nativity.

LANGSTON HUGHES

People who are brought face to face with the
infinite mystery of this holy Christmas night that
makes all races one become conscious that what
then happened was something immensely
important, something without parallel in the
history of mankind. The Nativity brings us within
touching distance, so to speak, of our spiritual birth
in God through grace.

POPE JOHN PAUL II

So if a Christian is touched only once a year,
the touching is still worth it, and maybe on some
given Christmas, some quiet morning, the touch
will take. Because the one message of Christmas is
the Christmas story. If it is false, we are doomed. If
it is true, as it must be, it makes everything else in
the world all right.

HARRY REASONER

To thee, meek majesty, soft King
  Of simple graces, and sweet loves!
Each of us his lamb will bring,
  Each his pair of silver doves!

RICHARD CRASHAW

Every Sunday now the Christ-child story was
told over and grew near and brighter like the
Christmas star. Mathew had not known about it
before, except that on a certain day in the year his
father had brought him toys. . . . Now he was
wrapped up in the story of love and sacrifice, and
felt his heart grow larger as he breathed it in,
looking on clear windless nights to see if he might
discern the Star of Bethlehem rising over pine
mountain and the Christ-child come walking on
the snow. It was not that he really expected it, but
that the story was so alive in him.

MARY AUSTIN

Born a King on Bethlehem's plain
Gold I bring to crown him again,
King forever, ceasing never
Over us all to reign.

Frankincense to offer have I,
Incense owns a Deity nigh:
Prayer and praising, all men raising,
Worship him, God on high.

Myrrh is mine; its bitter perfume
Breathes a life of gathering gloom;
Sorrowing, sighing, bleeding, dying,
Sealed in the stone cold tomb.

O star of wonder, star of night,
Star with royal beauty bright,
Westward leading, still proceeding,
Guide us to thy perfect light.

JOHN HENRY HOPKINS JR.

No love that in a family dwells,
    No carolling in frosty air,
Nor all the steeple-shaking bells
    Can with this single Truth compare—
That God was Man in Palestine
    And lives today in Bread and Wine.

JOHN BETJEMAN

hat can I give Him
  Poor as I am?
If I were a shepherd
  I would bring a lamb,
If I were a wise man
  I would do my part—
Yet what can I give him?
  Give my heart.

CHRISTINA ROSSETTI

A Frosty Christmas-eve '/when the stars were
    shining
Fared I forth alone '/where westward falls the hill
And from many a village '/in the water'd valley
Distant music reached me '/peals of bells a-ringing:
The constellated sounds '/ran sprinkling on earth's
    floor
As the dark vault above '/with stars was spangled
    o'er.

Then sped my thought to keep '/that first
    Christmas of all
When the shepherds watching '/by their folds ere
    the dawn
Heard music in the fields '/and marvelling could
    not tell
Whether it were angels '/or the bright stars singing.

ROBERT BRIDGES

Bid our peace increase,
  Thou that madest morn;
Bid oppressions cease,
Bid the night be peace,
  Bid the day be born.

ALGERNON CHARLES SWINBURNE

This happy day, whose risen sun
Shall not set through eternity,
This holy day when Christ the Lord,
Took on Him our humanity.

PHOEBE CARY

The shepherds sing; and shall I silent be?
  My God no hymn for thee?
My soul's a shepherd too; a flock it feeds
  Of thoughts and words and deeds;
My pasture is Thy Word; the streams Thy grace,
  Enriching all the place.

GEORGE HERBERT

Three Kings came riding from far away,
Melchior and Gaspar and Baltasar;
Three Wise Men out of the East were they,
And they traveled by night and slept by day,
For their guide was a beautiful, wonderful star.

HENRY WADSWORTH LONGFELLOW

A child this day is born,
A child of high reknown,
Most worthy of a sceptre,
A sceptre and a crown:
Nowell, Nowell, Nowell,
Nowell, sing all we may,
Because the King of all kings
Was born this blessed day.

OLD ENGLISH CAROL

We three kings of Orient are;
Bearing gifts we traverse afar
   Field and fountain,
   Moor and mountain,
Following yonder star:

O Star of wonder, star of night,
Star with royal beauty bright,
   Westward leading,
   Still proceeding,
Guide us to thy perfect light.

JOHN HENRY HOPKINS JR.

And when they were come into the house,
they saw the young child with Mary his mother,
and fell down, and worshipped him: and when they
had opened their treasures they presented unto him
gifts; gold, and frankincense, and myrrh.

SAINT MATTHEW

55

Lord, underneath the great blue sky,
   My heart shall paean sing,
The gold and myrrh of meekest love
   Mine only offering.

ALICE BROWN

. . . In a little while the entire sky from the Mount of Olives in the East to the Great Sea in the West was filled with what looked like Seraphim, with outspread wings; for as everybody knows, I hope, the Seraphim, which are the highest order of angelic beings, are red—burning with love. And in between the red Seraphim were blue spaces which it was easy to imagine were Cherubim, for, as everybody knows, I am sure, Cherubim are always blue, and are the supreme knowers, "the great Intelligences," beholding the truth with their minds. Here just above our heads, on the Shepherd's Field, on Christmas Eve, was a sky full of what looked to us like Seraphim and Cherubim. We beheld it with awe and wonder, and though we heard no words from above, we said in our hearts "Glory to God in the highest."

RUFUS M. JONES

And all new matters of ages to come
Arose as a vision of wonder in space.
All thoughts of ages, all dreams, new worlds,
All the future of galleries and museums,
All the games of fairies, the work of inventors,
The yule trees, and the dreams all children dream,
The tremulous glow of candles in rows,
The gold and silver of angels and globes
(A wind blew, raging, long from the plain)
And the splendor of tinsel and toys under trees.

BORIS PASTERNAK
Translated by Eugene M. Kayden.

III

THE HOLLY AND THE IVY

The holly and the ivy,
When they are both full grown,
Of all the trees that are in the wood,
The holly bears the crown.

We bring in the holly, the ivy, the pine,
The spruce and the hemlock together we twine;
With evergreen branches our walls we array
For the keeping of Christmas, our high holiday.
Glory to God in the highest we sing,
Peace and good-will are the tidings we bring.

OLD ENGLISH CAROL

"Six green branches we leave with you;
See they be scattered your house-place through.
"This staunch blithe Holly your board shall grace.
Mistletoe bless your chimney place,
"Laurel to crown your lighted hall,
Over your bed let the Yew-bough fall,
"Close by the cradle the Christmas Fir,
For elfin dreams in its branches stir.
"Last and loveliest, high and low,
From ceil to floor let the Ivy go."
From each glad guest I received my gift
And then the latch of my door did lift—
"Green singers, God prosper the song ye make
As ye sing to the world for Christ's sweet Sake."

ELEANOR FARJEON

Then sing to the holly, the Christmas holly,
    That hangs over peasant and king.

ELIZA COOK

61

But give me holly, bold and jolly,
Honest, prickly, shining holly;
Pluck me holly leaf and berry
For the day when I make merry.

CHRISTINA ROSSETTI

The holly was not in sprigs, but in enormous
branches, that filled the eye with the glistening
green and red; and in the embrasure of the front
window stood a young holly-tree entire, eighteen
feet high, and gorgeous with five hundred branches
of red berries. The tree had been dug up, and
planted here in an enormous bucket, used for that
purpose. . . .

CHARLES READE

Each house is swept the day before
And windows stuck with evergreens;
The snow is besomed from the door
And comfort crowns the cottage scenes.
Gilt holly with its thorny pricks
And yew and box with berries small,
These deck the unused candlesticks,
And pictures hanging by the wall.

JOHN CLARE

Miss Piggy hangs two hundred sprigs of
mistletoe—and I try to avoid them.

KERMIT THE FROG

From the center of the ceiling . . . old Wardle had just suspended, with his own hands, a huge branch of mistletoe, and this same branch of mistletoe instantaneously gave rise to a scene of general and most delightful scrambling and confusion; in the midst of which, Mr. Pickwick with a gallantry that would have done honour to a descendant of Lady Tollimglower herself, took the old lady by the hand, led her beneath the mystic branch, and saluted her in all courtesy and decorum. The old lady submitted to this piece of practical politeness with all the dignity that befitted so important and serious a solemnity, but the younger ladies not being so thoroughly imbued with a superstitious veneration for the custom: or imagining that the value of a salute is very much enhanced if it cost a little trouble to obtain it: screamed and struggled, and ran into corners, and threatened and remonstrated, and did everything but leave the room, until some of the less adventurous gentlemen were on the point of desisting, when they all at once found it useless to resist any longer, and submitted to be kissed with a good grace.

CHARLES DICKENS

I know that sprig of Mistletoe, O Spirit in the midst! Under it I swung the girl I loved—girl no more now than I am boy—and kissed her spite of blush and pretty shriek.

ALEXANDER SMITH

Within the hall are song and laughter
    The cheeks of Christmas glow red and jolly
And sprouting is every corbel and rafter
    With lightsome green of ivy and holly;
Through the deep gulf of the chimney wide
Wallows the Yule log's roaring tide.

JAMES RUSSELL LOWELL

Heap the holly! Wreath the pine!
Train the dainty Christmas vine—
Let the breath of fir and bay
Mingle on this festal day—
Let the cedar fill the air
With its spicy sweetness rare.
Wake the carol—sound the chime—
Welcome! Merry Christmas Time!

HELEN CHASE

My idea of decorating the house for Christmas
is to light up the rooftop with bright strings of
bulbs, drape garlands of greenery from pillar to post,
flash spots of bauble-studded trees, garnish the
garage door with a life-sized Santa Claus, and perch
a small elf on the mailbox that says "Y-U-L-E"
where his teeth should be.

My husband's idea of decorating for Christmas
is to replace the forty-watt bulb in the porch light
with a sixty-watter.

ERMA BOMBECK

With holly and ivy
    So green and so gay,
We deck up our houses
    As fresh as the day
With bays and rosemary,
    And laurel complete,
And everyone now
    Is a king in conceit.

POOR RICHARD'S ALMANACK

Again at Christmas did we weave
The holly round the Christmas hearth
The silent snow possessed the earth
And calmly fell our Christmas Eve.

ALFRED, LORD TENNYSON

The men had come back from their work on
shore with branches of green pine and holly, and
the women had stuck them about the ship, not
without tearful thoughts of old home places, where
their childhood fathers and mothers did the same.
    Bits and snatches of Christmas carols were
floating all around the ship, like land-birds blown
far out to sea.

HARRIET BEECHER STOWE
*describing the first American
Christmas of the Pilgrims.*

With garlands proper to the times
    Our doors are wreathed, our lintels strewn.
From our two steeples sound the chimes,
    Incessant, through the afternoon,
    Only a little out of tune.

Phyllis McGinley

Sitting under the mistletoe
(Pale-green, fairy mistletoe),
One last candle burning low,
All the sleepy dancers gone,
Just one candle burning on,
Shadows lurking everywhere:
Some one came, and kissed me there.

Tired I was, my head would go
Nodding under the mistletoe
(Pale-green, fairy mistletoe),
No footsteps came, no voice, but only,
Just as I sat there, sleepy, lonely,
Stopped in the still and shadowy air
Lips unseen—and kissed me there.

Walter de la Mare

look   the spangles
that sleep all year in a dark box
dreaming of being taken out and allowed to shine
the balls the chains red and gold fluffy threads

E. E. Cummings

In summer
sun,
in winter snow,
A dress of
green
you always
show.
O Christmas
tree,
O Christmas
tree,
How lovely
are
Your branches.

Choose
wisely then,
each ornament
And frosted
tinsel skein
For branches
that have
worn jewels
Of gleaming
mountain rain.

OLD ENGLISH VARIATION
of "O Tannenbaum"

ELIZABETH ELLEN LONG

I did not know she'd take it so,
    Or else I'd never dared:
Although the bliss was worth the blow,
I did not know she'd take it so.
She stood beneath the mistletoe
So long I thought she cared;
I did not know she'd take it so,
    Or else I'd never dared.

COUNTEE CULLEN

any men look out at gray December skies and think of the time when they helped get the Christmas tree. The day before Christmas Father was likely to say after breakfast, "Son, let's take our axes and go up to the wood lot. Mother and the girls will want to trim the tree this evening."

. . . Among the cedars, spruces, and hemlocks all was peaceful and quiet. It was as if they entered a world where strife and man-made problems were unknown. There was a gentle murmuring among the branches overhead. The air was filled with the tangy, invigorating fragrance of the evergreens.

Haydn S. Pearson

In California, now, our tree still comes from the woods where I was a boy, trucked two thousand miles, not two thousand yards. It's taller now, because our ceiling's higher. But I don't get to go out in the dark, snowy woods on a winter afternoon and watch it fall, crashing in a cloud of snow for Christmas. I can't sit through Christmas afternoon behind the tree in a window seat, devouring my Christmas books. My first copies of *Treasure Island* and *Huckleberry Finn* still have some blue-spruce needles scattered in the pages. They smell of Christmas still.

Charlton Heston

68

O hemlock tree! O hemlock tree!
How faithful are thy branches!
   Green not alone in summer time,
   But in the winter's frost and rime!
O Tannenbaum! O Tannenbaum!
How faithful are thy branches!

TRADITIONAL GERMAN CAROL

. . . I'd read about 'em having Christmas
trees, and I went down the creek way a piece. I'us
looking for an evergreen, and I couldn't find one,
so I cut a sourwood tree—had all the tags still
hanging on it, and I decorated it with red ribbon,
red paper, popcorn, and red apples. It pleased the
children so well that they've had a Christmas tree
ever since.

MOM RITCHIE
mother of folk-singer
June Ritchie.

Now gay trees rise
Before your eyes,
Abloom with tempting cheer;
Blithe voices sing
And blithe bells ring
For Christmastide
Is here.

OLD ENGLISH CAROL

O balsam tree, that lately held
The stars like nestling birds among
Your emerald branches, listen now
To children's voices sweet with song.

FRANCES FROST

Trees just do not grow on the high plateaus of
the Rockies. Everybody knows that. Trees need
good soil and good weather and up here there's no
soil and terrible weather. That's why the tree is a
kind of miracle.

The tree is a juniper, and it grows beside U.S.
Route 50 utterly alone. Nobody remembers who
put the first Christmas ornament on it—some
whimsical motorist of years ago. From that day to
this, the tree has been redecorated each year.
Nobody knows who does it. But each year, by
Christmas Day, the tree has become a Christmas
tree.

CHARLES KURALT

When I'm looking at a well-decorated
Christmas tree, no amount of adverse experience
can convince me that people are anything but good.
If people were bad, they wouldn't go to all that
trouble to display that much affection for one
another and the world they live in.

ANDY ROONEY

The secret of the best Christmases is
everybody doing the same things all at the same
time. You will all fall to and string cranberries and
popcorn for the tree, and the bright lines each of
you has a hold on will radiate from the tree like
ribbons on a maypole.

ROBERT P. TRISTRAM COFFIN

. . . there was a round iron stove, a very jolly
stove, a cozy stove that winked at you with its red
isin-glass eyes. On top of this stove was a round
iron plate, it was flat, and a wonderful place to pop
corn. There was a copper kettle, used for making
maple syrup, and we shook the popper on the top of
the stove. . . . The corn popped, and we poured it
into the kettle and emptied the kettle, and poured
it full again, until there was a whole barrel-full of
popcorn, as white and fluffy as the snow that
carpeted the lawn between the parsonage and the
church.

Then we got out a darning needle, a big one,
and a ball of string. We strung the popcorn into
long, long ropes, to hang upon the tree. But that
was only half of it! There were stars to be cut out of
kindergarten paper, red and green, and silver, and
gold, and walnuts to be wrapped in gold paper. . . .
And red apples to be polished, because a shiny apple
makes a brave show on a tree. And when it was all
finished, it was Christmas Eve.

DOROTHY THOMPSON

I have been looking on, this evening, at a merry company of children assembled round that pretty German toy, a Christmas tree. The tree was planted in the middle of a great round table, and towered high above their heads. It was brilliantly lighted by a multitude of little tapers; and everywhere sparkled and glittered with bright objects. There were rosy-cheeked dolls, hiding behind the green leaves; and there were real watches (with movable hands, at least, and an endless capacity of being wound up) dangling from innumerable twigs; there were French-polished tables, chairs, bedsteads, wardrobes, eight day clocks, and various other articles of domestic furniture (wonderfully made, in tin, at Wolverhampton), perched among the boughs, as if in preparation for some fairy housekeeping; there were jolly broadfaced men, more agreeable in appearance than many real men—and no wonder, for their heads took off, and showed them to be full of sugar-plums; there were fiddles and drums . . . there were trinkets for the elder girls, far brighter than any grown-up gold and jewels . . . imitation apples, pears and walnuts, crammed with surprises . . . in short, as a pretty child delightedly whispered to another pretty child, "There was everything, and more."

Charles Dickens

. . . And the fir tree was put into a great tub filled with sand; but no one could see that it was a tub, for it was hung round with green cloth, and stood on a large, many-colored carpet. Oh, how the tree trembled! What was to happen now? The servants, and the young ladies also, decked it out. On one branch they hung little nets, cut out of colored paper; every net was filled with sweetmeats; golden apples and walnuts hung down, as if they grew there, and more than a hundred little candles, red, white and blue, were fastened to the different boughs. Dolls that looked exactly like real people— the Tree had never seen such before—swung among the foliage, and high on the summit of the Tree was fixed a tinsel star. It was splendid, particularly splendid.

HANS CHRISTIAN ANDERSEN

Each time we've moved, our Christmas box, labeled "Priceless," has moved with us. The accumulated ornaments, handmade and store-bought, recount times of our lives and places we have lived. The Christmas tree, for us, is another kind of family record. Uncovering the boxes of decorations is like opening a wonderful old book, and, as we dress the tree, we reread our past.

HOLLY HOBBIE

My flair for decorating comes out when the tree is to be trimmed. *Moi,* I am a traditionalist. I use candy canes, cookies, strings of corncobs and a teensy photo of myself for the top. It seems appropriate that the star at the top of my tree is *moi.*

MISS PIGGY

And what a tree! Of just the right size for the room, it had a shape and symmetry that surely no other tree in all Christmasdom could equal. It tapered gradually with exquisite shape and form to a point that quivered and flickered like a green flame. On the flame sturdily triumphed Father Christmas, diminutive in body, but alive in his smile, his stolidity, his gallant colour. It was the colour that entranced the eye. . . . The thin chains of frosted silver that hung from bough to bough seemed of themselves to dance in patterned rhythm. Balls of fire, emerald and ruby, amethyst and crystal, shone in the light of the candles. The light that flashed from its boughs was not foreign to it, but seemed to be, integrally, part of its life and history. . . . The candles seemed to be the voice of the tree; it was vocal in its pleasure, its sense of fun at its own splendour, its grand surprise that it had after all come off so well.

HUGH WALPOLE

74

About December twenty-first the tree things
are brought down from the attic. This has
happened so often in this and other houses you'd
think they could spill from the cartons and boxes
and climb down the attic ladder by themselves. It's
an interesting fancy—the birds flying, some with
only one wing; the round colored globes bouncing
(but not breaking); and all the tree angels
marching—or winging—in pairs.

FAITH BALDWIN

Put out the lights now!
Look at the Tree, the rough tree dazzled
In oriole plumes of flame,
Tinselled with twinkling frost fire, tasselled
With stars and moons—the same
That yesterday hid in the spinney and had no fame
Til we put out the lights now.

CECIL DAY-LEWIS

IV

Their
old
Familiar
Carols Play

I heard the bells on Christmas day,
Their old familiar carols play,
And wild and sweet the words repeat,
Of peace on earth,
Good will to men.

Willie, take your little drum,
With your whistle, Robin, come!
  When we hear the fife and drum,
Tu-re-lu-re-lu, pat-a-pat-a-pan,
    When we heard the fife and drum,
    Christmas should be frolicsome.

<small>OLD ENGLISH SONG</small>

Sound over all waters, reach out from all lands,
The chorus of voices, the clasping of hands;
Sing hymns that were sung by the stars of the
  morn,
Sing songs of the angels when Jesus was born!
  With glad jubilations
  Bring hope to the nations!
The dark night is ending and dawn has begun:
Rise, hope of the ages, arise like the sun,
  All speech flow to music, all hearts beat as one!

<small>JOHN GREENLEAF WHITTIER</small>

If it is dark, you
cannot see
the horses curvetting
and prancing,
but you would know
to hear those bells
that those who
shook them
must be dancing.

<small>ELIZABETH COATSWORTH</small>

79

Wassail, wassail, all over the town!
Our toast it is white, and our ale it is brown,
Our bowl it is made of the white maple tree;
With the wassailing bowl, we'll drink to thee.

So here is to Cherry and to his right cheek,
Pray God send our master a good piece of beef,
And a good piece of beef that may we all see;
With the wassailing bowl, we'll drink to thee.

And here is to Dobbin and to his right eye,
Pray God send our master a good Christmas pie,
And a good Christmas pie that may we all see;
With our wassailing bowl we'll drink to thee.

And here is to Fillpail and to her left ear,
Pray God send our master a happy New Year,
And a happy New Year as e'er he did see;
With our wassailing bowl we'll drink to thee.

Come, butler, come fill us a bowl of the best,
Then we hope that your soul in heaven may rest;
But if you do draw us a bowl of the small,
Then down shall go butler, bowl and all.

Then here's to the maid in the lily white smock,
Who tripped to the door and slipped back the lock!
Who tripped to the door and pulled back the pin,
For to let these jolly wassailers in.

Traditional English
Wassailing Song

Blow bugles of battle, the marches of peace;
East, west, north and south, let the long
    quarrel cease;
Sing the song of great joy that the angels
    began,
Sing of glory to God and of good-will
    to man!

JOHN GREENLEAF WHITTIER

Sweeter is ne'er the bells ringing
Than at Christmas time.
'Tis as if angels were singing,
Singing of the good-will sublime!
Singing again as in yon blessed night
Bells, with your holiest chime,
Sing for all people and time.

NORTH GERMAN SONG

Wisselton, wasselton, who lives here?
We've come to taste your Christmas beer.
Up the kitchen and down the hall,
Holly, ivy and mistletoe;
A peck of apples will serve us all,
Give us some apples and let us go.

Up with your stocking, on with your shoe,
If you haven't any apples, money will do.
My carol's done, and I must be gone,
No longer can I stay here.
God bless you all, great and small,
And send you a happy new year.

TRADITIONAL ENGLISH

81

On the corner, get together,
Sing a Christmas song, as we swing along
Through the cold and snowy weather,
Marching up and down around the town.

Merry Christmas! Merry Christmas!
Merry Christmas to all and a happy New Year!
Join the happy crowd, lift your voices loud,
And we'll soon find you a cup of cheer!

Here's a toast to you all:
Now may God rest you merry, gentlemen!
Another year, we'll gather here,
And then we'll be toasting you again.

Traditional French-Canadian

Villagers all, this frosty tide,
Let your doors swing open wide,
Though wind may follow, and snow beside,
Yet draw us in by your fire to bide;
    Joy shall be yours in the morning!

Here we stand in the cold and the sleet,
Blowing fingers and stamping feet,
Come from far away you to greet—
You by the fire and we in the street—
    Bidding you joy in the morning!

Old English Carol

Here we come a-wassailing
Among the leaves so green,
Here we come a-wandering,
So fair to be seen:

We are not daily beggars
That beg from door to door,
But we are neighbours' children
Whom you have seen before:

Call up the butler of this house,
Put on his golden ring;
Let him bring us up a glass of beer,
And better shall we sing:

We have got a little purse
Of stretching leather skin;
We want a little of your money
To line it well within:

Bring us out a table,
And spread it with a cloth;
Bring us out a mouldy cheese,
And some of your Christmas loaf:

God bless the master of this house,
Likewise the mistress too;
And all the little children
That round the table go.

Good Master and good mistress,
While you're sitting by your fire,
Pray think of us poor children
Who are wand'ring in the mire.

TRADITIONAL ENGLISH
WASSAILING SONG

At the break of Christmas Day,
Through the frosty starlight ringing,
Faint and sweet and far away,
Comes the sound of children, singing,
Chanting, singing,
"Cease to mourn
For Christ is born
Peace and joy to all men bringing!"

MARGARET DELAND

Everything was quiet; everywhere there was the faint crackling silence of the winter night. We started singing, and we were all moved by the words and the sudden trueness of our voices. Pure, very clear, and breathless we sang:
"As Joseph was a-walking
He heard an angel sing,
This night shall be the birth-time
Of Christ the Heavenly King. . . ."
And two thousand Christmases became real to us then; the houses, the halls, the places of paradise had all been visited; the stars were bright to guide the Kings through the snow; and across the farmyard we could hear the beasts in their stalls. We were given roast apples and hot mince pies, in our nostrils were spices like myrrh, and in our wooden box, as we headed back for the village, there were golden gifts for all.

LAURIE LEE

And singers too, a merry throng,
At early morn with simple skill
Yet imitate the angel's song
And chant their Christmas ditty still;
And 'mid the storm that dies and swells
By fits—in humming softly steals
The music of the village bells
Ringing round their merry peals.

JOHN CLARE

The time draws near the birth of Christ;
　The moon is hid; the night is still;
　The Christmas bells from hill to hill
Answer each other in the mist.

ALFRED, LORD TENNYSON

. . . the bells began to ring for the evening
service: first one, clear and high in the darkness;
then another, a deeper warmer one; and soon all
eight fell into their places in the scale. Over and
over they tumbled down the length of the scale
until there was no beginning and no ending to it,
but just a continuous flow like water down a long
waterfall. And then the bells suddenly changed
places and wove in and out of one another on a new
tune.

MARTIN ARMSTRONG

Dashing through the snow,
In a one-horse open sleigh,
O'er the fields we go,
Laughing all the way;
Bells on bobtail ring,
Making spirits bright,
What fun it is to ride and sing
A sleighing song tonight!

Jingle bells, jingle bells,
Jingle all the way!
Oh, what fun it is to ride
In a one-horse open sleigh!

JOHN PIERPONT

The snow turned all to pearl, the dark trees strung with pearls, the sky beginning to glow with such a radiance as never was on land or sea. And the stillness everywhere; the live vibrant stillness of just before a great orchestra begins to play, or angels to sing.

GLADYS HASTY CARROLL

What sweeter music can we bring
Than a carol for to sing
The birth of this our heav'nly King?
Awake the voice! Awake the string!

ROBERT HERRICK

Ring out, ye crystal spheres!
Once bless our human ears,
    If ye have power to touch our senses so;
And let your silver chime
Move in melodious time,
    And let the bass of Heaven's deep organ blow,
And with your manifold harmony
Make up full consort to the angelic symphony.

JOHN MILTON

Hark! The Herald Angels Sing
Glory to the new-born King!
Peace on earth and mercy mild,
God and sinners reconciled.
Joyful all ye nations rise,
Join the triumph of the skies;
With angelic host proclaim,
Christ is born in Bethlehem.
Hark! The Herald Angels Sing
Glory to the new-born King!

CHARLES WESLEY

Over earth's shadows are ringing yet
    The notes of celestial song;
The voices of angles and men are met,
    And praises high prolong;
        Oh, love untold,
        Hope manifold,
Joy of each Christmas morn!

ANONYMOUS

I went to midnight Mass for the first time
when I was 16, moving through the frigid night in
the backseat of a car, smug in my black velvet dress
and camel's hair coat. Like the hallways at school
when we were there for a dance, the church looked
out of place and time at night, the reds and blues of
the stained glass windows colorless and flat in the
dark. But the candles made an oasis within. There
was a great, deep silence when the bells rang twelve,
the kind of silence there is supposed to be in church
but rarely is, and then the soprano voices: O come,
all ye faithful.

ANNA QUINDLEN

Now all the people knew that at the top of the
tower was a chime of Christmas bells. They had
hung there ever since the church was built, and
were the most beautiful bells in the world. Some
thought it was because a great musician had cast
them and arranged them in their place; others said
it was because of the great height, which reached up
to where the air was clearest and purest; however
that might be, no one who had ever heard the
chimes denied that they were the sweetest in the
world. Some described them as sounding like angels
far up in the sky; others, as sounding like strange
winds singing through the trees.

RAYMOND MACDONALD ALDEN

It *is* the calm and silent night!
  A thousand bells ring out, and throw
Their joyous peals abroad, and smite
  The darkness, charm'd and holy now.

Alfred Domett

High in the steeple the bells were conversing. Two of the younger ones were vexed and spoke angrily, "Is it not time we were asleep? It is almost midnight, and twice we have been shaken, twice we have been forced to cry out through the gloom just as though it were day, and we were singing the call for Sunday Mass. There are people moving about in the Church; are we going to be tormented again, I wonder? Might they not leave us in peace?"

At this the oldest bell in the steeple said indignantly, in a voice which though cracked had lost none of its solemnity, "Hush, little ones! Are you not ashamed to speak so foolishly? When you went to Rome to be blessed, did you not take an oath, did you not swear to fulfill your duty? Do you not know that in a few minutes it will be Christmas, and that you will then celebrate the birth of him whose resurrection you have already celebrated? The clock is about to strike the hour— now—Christmas! Christmas! Ring out with all your heart and all your might! Let no man say that he has not been summoned to midnight Mass."

Maxime Du Camp

News of a fair and marvelous thing,
  The snow in the streets, and the wind on
    the door,
Nowell, Nowell, Nowell, we sing.
  Minstrels and maids stand forth on the
    floor.
  From far away we come to you,
  To tell of great tidings, strange and
    true.

WILLIAM MORRIS

O Come, all ye faithful,
Joyful and triumphant,
O come ye, O come ye to Bethlehem;
Come and behold Him,
Born the King of Angels;
O come, let us adore Him,
O come, let us adore Him,
O come, let us adore Him,
Christ the Lord!

TRADITIONAL

Mortals, your homage be gratefully bringing,
And sweet let the gladsome hosanna arise:
Ye angels, the full alleluia be singing;
One chorus resound through the earth and the
  skies.

WILLIAM A. MUHLENBERG

We ring
the bells
on Christmas Day
Oh, why?
Oh, why?
To Echo what
the angels say
On high!
On High!

ELSIE WILLIAMS CHANDLER

The irruption of this motley crew, with
beat of drum, according to ancient custom, was the
consummation of uproar and merriment. Master
Simon covered himself with glory by the stateliness
with which, as Ancient Christmas, he walked a
minuet with the peerless, though giggling, Dame
Mince Pie. It was followed by a dance of all the
characters, which from its medley of costumes,
seemed as though the old family portraits had
skipped down from their frames to join in the sport.
Different centuries were figuring at cross hands
right and left; the dark ages were cutting pirouettes
and rigadoons; and the days of Queen Bess jigging
merrily down the middle, through a line of
succeeding generations.

WASHINGTON IRVING

Julie had promised that it would be the best Christmas ever, and it was. I realized suddenly why it always is. Christmas is cumulative. Whatever else it has lost, every year which has passed since the birth of Christ has retained and added to the magic of light and color against a dark background, to the human capacity for appreciation of chords and bells and melodies, to the sweetness of children's voices. . . .

GLADYS HASTY CARROLL

ngels we have heard on high,
　　Sweetly singing o'er the plains,
　　And the mountains in reply,
　　Echoing their joyous strains
　　　　Gloria in excelsis Deo.

Shepherds, why this jubilee
Why your joyous strains prolong?
What the gladsome tidings be
Which inspire your heav'nly song?
　　　Gloria in excelsis Deo.

Come to Bethlehem and see
Him whose birth the angels sing;
Come, adore on bended knee,
Christ the Lord, the newborn King.
　　　Gloria in excelsis Deo.

TRADITIONAL FRENCH

. . . there was a gentle tap at the bay window. Mr. Raby went and threw it open, and immediately a woman's voice, clear and ringing, sang outside—

"The first Noel the angels did say,
Was to three poor shepherds in fields as they
lay. . . ."

As the Noel proceeded, some came in at the window, others at the doors, and the lower part of the room began to fill with singers and auditors.

The Noel ended, there was a silence, during which the organ was opened, the bellows blown, and a number of servants and others came into the room with little lighted tapers, and stood in a long row, awaiting a signal from the Squire.

He took out his watch and, finding it was close on twelve o'clock, directed the doors to be flung open, that he might hear the great clock in the hall strike the quarters.

The clock struck the first quarter—dead silence; the second—the third—dead silence.

But at the fourth, and with the first stroke of midnight, out burst the full organ and fifty voices, with the *Gloria in excelsis Deo;* and, as that divine hymn surged on, the lighters ran along the walls and lighted the eighty candles, and, for the first time, the twelve waxen pillars, so that, as the hymn concluded, the room was in a blaze, and it was Christmas Day.

CHARLES READE

Oh, children of the village choir,
  Your carols on the midnight throw!
Oh, bright across the mist and mire,
  Ye ruddy hearths of Christmas glow!

ANDREW LANG

On Christmas-eve the bells were rung;
The damsel donned her kirtle sheen;
The hall was dressed with holly green;
Forth to the wood did merry men go,
To gather in the mistletoe.
Thus opened wide the baron's hall
To vassal, tenant, serf and all;
Power laid his rod of rule aside
And ceremony doffed his pride.
The heir, with roses in his shoes,
That night might village partner choose;
The lord, underogating, share
The vulgar game of "Post and Pair."
All hailed, with uncontrolled delight,
And general voice, the happy night
That to the cottage, as the crown,
Brought tidings of salvation down.

SIR WALTER SCOTT

We have heard the children say—
    Gentle children, whom we love—
Long ago on Christmas Day,
    Came a message from above.

Still, as Christmas-tide comes round,
    They remember it again
Echo still the joyful sound
    "Peace on earth, good-will to men!"

Yet the hearts must child-like be
    Where such heavenly guests abide;
Unto children, in their glee,
    All the year is Christmas-tide!

LEWIS CARROLL

V

JOLLY OLD SAINT NICHOLAS

Jolly old Saint Nicholas
Lean your ear this way;
Don't you tell a single soul
What I'm going to say:
Christmas Eve is coming soon;
Now you dear old man,
Whisper what you'll bring to me,
Tell me if you can.

Here comes old Father Christmas
With sound of fife and drums;
With mistletoe about his brows,
So merrily he comes!

ROSE TERRY COOKE

any of you have complained about the
severity of our laughing course. We realize how
difficult it is these days to produce a good
convincing "Ho, Ho, Ho!" when we all feel such a
powerful urge to sit down and cry. We can only
suggest that you stop reading the newspapers for
the next month.

Many of you will note that a long series of
"Ho, ho, ho's" will bring on a spasm of racking
coughs, particularly if the little visitor is pressing an
elbow into your breastbone. In these cases a switch
to "Hah, hah, hah" usually relieves the problem. In
no case, however, should you let out a "Heh, heh,
heh." Most merchandizers feel that "Heh, heh,
heh" is extremely harmful to the store image.

RUSSELL BAKER

Miss Manners is extremely sorry to report that the two most frequently asked questions about the charming custom of giving and receiving Christmas presents are: (1) Do I have to get them something? and (2) How can I make people give me what I really want? These questions shouldn't even be thought, much less asked.

JUDITH MARTIN

I saw Mommy kissing Santa Claus
underneath the mistletoe last night. . . .
Oh, what a laugh it would have been,
if Daddy had only seen
Mommy kissing Santa Claus last night.

TOMMIE CONNER

The Christmas season is getting off to an unorthodox start in a lot of places, it seems. The Holiday Photo and Display company of Chicago says it was justified in not hiring Cynthia Larson, who has filed a sex discrimination complaint against the company. Miss Larson, who is nineteen, had applied for the job of Santa Claus. Company president Robert Heiss says that the two men hired for the job were of the more boisterous Ho Ho Ho types people expect Santa Claus to be. Miss Larson was hired as a Santa's helper, but filed the complaint anyway, maintaining that in order to go Ho Ho Ho you don't have to be a he he he.

CHARLES OSGOOD

Johnny wants a pair of skates
    Susy wants a sled;
Nellie wants a picture book;
    Yellow, blue and red;
Now I think I'll leave to you
    What to give the rest;
Choose for me, dear Santa Claus
    You will know the best.

TRADITIONAL

hirty days hath September
April, June, and November;
When December doth arrive
Kids can't count past "25."

H. J. HIGDON

The twelfth day of Christmas
My true love sent to me
Twelve fiddlers fiddling,
Eleven ladies dancing,
Ten pipers piping
Nine drummers drumming,
Eight maids a-milking,
Seven swans a-swimming
Six geese a-laying
Five gold rings,
Four colly birds,
Three French hens
Two turtle doves, and
A partridge in a pear tree.

TRADITIONAL

On Christmas Eve when I was twelve, I got a
mysterious call from my Dad asking me to meet
him at his office. I got there, he handed me a
burlap bag, and out slithered an eleven-foot bull
snake—believe it or not, just what I wanted! His
secretary fainted, and my mother wasn't exactly
overjoyed. I began to understand why my present
wasn't under the tree with all the other gifts.

MICHAEL DOUGLAS

Then when I was around five, with a child's
acuity of vision, I went to a Christmas party at a
friend's house and Santa Claus was there. I looked
up at him. But already my suspicions were aroused.
It seemed this Santa Claus talked exactly like Mr.
Lewis—he had a wheezing voice—he walked
exactly like Mr. Lewis and I knew he was Mr.
Lewis, who was my friend's father. How did he get
into Santa's clothes? Why would he make out like
Santa Claus at a party? So that day, after brooding
for a long time, I told my mother and father, I
think Santa Claus is parents. With a great leap of
logic, I understood why Santa Claus gave rich
people big presents and poor people little or none,
things like apples and oranges or, worst of all,
"useful clothes." Although it did not explain the
rich and the poor, it explained why a bad rich child
like Sport Richards, who kicked me when I was
waiting in line at school, had a grand Santa Claus
while another, poor child I knew had *shoes* for
Christmas.

CARSON MCCULLERS

102

A bird on Bellows
A Cuckoo
A turnabout Parrot
A Grocer's Shop
An Aviary
A Prussian Dragoon
A Man Smoakg
A Tunbridge Tea Sett
3 Neat Tunbridge Toys
A Neat Book fash Tea Chest
A box best Household Stuff
A straw Patch box w. a Glass
A neat dress'd Wax Baby

GEORGE WASHINGTON
1759 Christmas list for his
stepchildren, then five
and three.

Most all the time, the whole year
    round, there ain't no flies on me.
But jest 'fore Christmas I'm as good
    as I kin be!

EUGENE FIELD

Some people like anything you give them
just because *you* gave it to them. Other people never
like anything you give them and there's nothing
you can do about it.

ANDY ROONEY

hen as Christmas Eve approached I was filled with anxious questioning as to how St. Nick could get into our house to fill our waiting stockings. There was no chimney down which he could slide safely; in fact, I finally decided that it was an absolute impossibility for him to fit into the house through any chimney it possessed. My concern on this matter reached such a pitch that I took it up with mother. I told her my fears and she said he would most certainly be able to leave his gifts, for when no large chimney was provided, the parents would leave the door open a crack, at least, so he could push his way in with no difficulty whatever. This was a most reasonable solution and I was fully satisfied, and later events proved that my faith in her explanation was justified.

HARRIET ADAMS
from Pioneer Women *by*
Joanna L. Stratton.

Dear Children, now that you are older, I will tell you a secret. No matter what anyone says, Santa Claus is not your parents. He is the parent we wish we were, riding high and free above your head, pulled by enchanted reindeer and bringing you presents that could never be less than perfect.

I believe in Santa, oh, yes, I believe.

JOAN GOULD

There were many children's parties at
Christmas with assorted Santas giving gifts. One
time, the man ho-hoing behind the spun-silver
beard was David Niven—an elegant, urbane Father
Christmas, a soigné Saint Nick. Another year,
Charlton Heston played him differently—a man of
unearthly substance and stature, his ho-hos
booming down from a great height, somewhere
between Santa Claus and God: when *he* asked if
you'd been good all year, it caused a real crisis of
conscience.

CANDACE BERGEN

'Twas the night before Christmas, when all through
    the house
Not a creature was stirring, not even a mouse.

CLEMENT C. MOORE

In Baltimore there lived a boy,
He wasn't anybody's joy.
Although his name was Jabez Dawes,
His character was full of flaws.
In school he never led his classes,
He hid old ladies' reading glasses,
His mouth was open while he chewed,
And elbows to the table glued.
He stole the milk of hungry kittens,
And walked through doors marked No Admittance.
He said he acted thus because
There wasn't any Santa Claus.

OGDEN NASH

The Eve is here, with merriment for all,
And Santa Claus, with merry marvels fraught,
  Before the dawn across the roofs comes
    stealing.

GELETT BURGESS

Yes, Virginia, there is a Santa Claus. He exists as certainly as love and generosity and devotion exist, and you know that they abound and give to your life its highest beauty and joy. Alas! how dreary would be the world if there were no Santa Claus! It would be as dreary as if there were no Virginias. There would be no childlike faith then, no poetry, no romance to make tolerable this existence. We should have no enjoyment, except in sense and sight. The eternal light with which childhood fills the world would be extinguished.

Not believe in Santa Claus! You might as well not believe in fairies! You might get your papa to hire men to watch in all the chimneys on Christmas Eve to catch Santa Claus, but even if they did not see Santa Claus coming down, what would that prove? Nobody sees Santa Claus, but that is no sign that there is no Santa Claus. The most real things in the world are those that neither children nor men can see. . . .

No Santa Claus! Thank God he lives, and he lives forever. A thousand years from now, Virginia, nay ten times ten thousand years from now, he will continue to make glad the heart of childhood.

FRANCIS P. CHURCH

I didn't believe her. Angels had better things
to do with their time than watch to see if I was a
good or bad boy. Even with my limited seven-year-
old wisdom I had figured out that, at best, the
Angel could only watch over two or three kids at a
time . . . and why should I be one of them? The
odds were certainly in my favor. Yet Mama, who
knew all things, had told me, time and time again,
that the Christmas Angel knew, saw and evaluated
all things and could not be compared with anything
we ignorant human beings understood. I wasn't at
all sure that I believed in the Christmas Angel. All
my friends in the neighborhood told me that it was
Santa Claus who came on Christmas Eve and that
they'd never heard of an Angel who brought
presents. Mama, who though she had lived in
America for many years and blessed her new land as
her permanent home, was forever as Italian as
polenta. "Who's this Santa Claus?" she'd say.
"And what has he to do with Christmas?"

LEO F. BUSCAGLIA

As I drew in my head and was turning around,
Down the chimney Saint Nicholas came with a
 bound.
He was dressed all in fur from his head to his foot,
And his clothes were all tarnished with ashes and
 soot;
A bundle of toys he had flung on his back,
And he looked like a peddler just opening his pack.

CLEMENT C. MOORE

. . . of all the beasts that begged to do him service, Claus liked the reindeer best. "You shall go with me in my travels, for henceforth I shall bear my treasures not only to the children of the North, but to the children in every land whither the star points me and where the cross is lifted up!" So said Claus to the reindeer, and the reindeer neighed joyously and stamped their hoofs impatiently, as though they longed to start immediately.

EUGENE FIELD

t was the night before Christmas
And all through the house
Not a creature was stirring.
Not even a mouse.
For like everyone else in that
house which was old
The poor mouse was in bed
with a miserable cold.

LUDWIG BEMELMANS

Now, Dasher! now, Dancer! now, Prancer, and
Vixen!
On, Comet! on, Cupid! on, Donder and Blitzen!—
To the top of the porch, to the top of the wall,
Now, dash away, dash away, dash away all!

CLEMENT C. MOORE

I have often found myself wondering what model household inspired the bard who penned the immortal lines, "And all through the house not a creature was stirring, not even a mouse." We used to stir until six in the morning. Once the tree had been trimmed (late), and the cartons opened (later), we began the real work of the night, which was to put together all the toys that had arrived in separate pieces. It has been explained to me that toys are packed in shards, to be assembled by the middle-aged and butter-fingered, because this makes it easier for the shippers. It has not been explained to my satisfaction.

JEAN KERR

. . . it must be remembered that the age of Santa Claus is not a withered, haggard misshapen age. It is hearty, robust, vigorous and well nourished. It has the aspect and the essence of immortal youth. Those rosy cheeks and that dancing belly are not the equipment of an ascetic who grudges to others the gaiety of life because he has long since lost his share in it. The saint has made merry through his thousand years and he proposes to keep it up with all the wisdom and variety of his long experience. Let silly youth and callow infancy think to outdo him: they will find themselves mistaken. And he rushes his gay and riotus movement through the wide, sparkling progress of the night, without cessation, and without fatigue.

GAMALIEL BRADFORD

Someone will decide to tidy up the place by putting all wrapping paper and ribbons in a big empty box that held a Christmas present a few hours earlier.

I don't do any of this because I love the mess. As soon as you clear up the living room, Christmas is over.

ANDY ROONEY

Then out of that perfumed darkness a voice sounded: "Come in if you wish to come in!"

And the voice was wonderful, big, deep, merry, kind—as though it had but one meaning, the love of the earth's children; it betokened almighty justice and impartiality to children. And it betrayed no surprise or resentment at being intruded upon. After a while it invited more persuasively: "Come in if you wish to come in."

And this time it seemed not so much to proceed from near the Tree as to emanate from the Tree itself—to be the Tree speaking!

The children of the house at once understood that the nature of their irruption had shifted. Their father in that disguised voice was issuing instructions that they were not to dare question the ancient Christmas rites of the house, nor attack his sacred office in them. For this hour he was still to be the Santa Claus of childish faith. Since they did not believe, they must make believe!

JAMES LANE ALLEN

Up on the housetop reindeer pause,
Out jumps good old Santa Claus;
Down thru the chimney with lots of toys,
All for the little ones, Christmas joys.

TRADITIONAL

One of my earliest memories is of a Christmas
morning when Santa Claus brought me some books
and a Shetland pony, and I couldn't read or ride
because I awoke with a case of the measles. Mama
forbade me to expose my eyes to any bright light. I
remember being caught curled up behind the sofa
in the front sitting room with one of the new
books. I was not too sick to get a spanking.

JIMMY CARTER

Wednesday, 25th December, 1805. We were
awakened at daylight by a discharge of firearms,
which was followed by a song from the men, as a
compliment to us on the return of Christmas,
which we have always been accustomed to observe
as a day of rejoicing. After breakfast we divided our
remaining stock of tobacco, which amounted to
twelve carrots, into two parts; one of which we
distributed among such of the party as made use of
it; making a present of a handkerchief to the
others. The remainder of the day was passed in
good spirits though there was nothing in our
situation to excite much gayety.

THE JOURNALS OF LEWIS AND CLARK

His eyes how they twinkled, his dimples how merry!
His cheeks were like roses, his nose like a cherry;
His droll little mouth was drawn up like a bow,
And the beard on his chin was as white as the
    snow;
The stump of a pipe he held tight in his teeth.
And the smoke, it encircled his head like a wreath.
He had a broad face, and a little round belly,
That shook when he laughed, like a bowl full of
    jelly.
He was chubby and plump—a right jolly old elf;
And I laughed when I saw him, in spite of myself.

CLEMENT C. MOORE

Christmas Eve: Stockings hung at the foot of
our beds—stockings to fit a giant—cut of white
felt with Santas and trees stitched here and there.
By the nursery hearth a bowl of milk and cookies
placed for Santa and his reindeer.
    Christmas Morning: Empty in the morning,
the almond cookies—vanished! In ecstasy stockings
are pounced on, silver and gold paper torn asunder
to reveal amazements . . . a walnut opening to an
elfin village sprinkled with crystals, a harmonica, a
mouse to wind and see it scurry across the room,
then on and on until at last—the toe is reached
and the fingers come upon the crinkly cool of a
globe the hand can barely hold; my nose squashes
against the sweet spice of it—a tangerine!—simple
as can be, the best surprise, the nicest one of all.

GLORIA VANDERBILT

As a kid, sometimes my Christmas present was an orange. We were real poor and fruit was a once-a-year thing. To this day that's why I *love* the smell of oranges.

DOLLY PARTON

They never opened their gifts all at the same time at Christmas. First one would open a package while the others watched, and then another, turn by turn, each thrilling to the thrill of giving and receiving, stretching the joy into many dove-tailed installments.

GEORGE V. MARTIN

Laura and Mary would never have looked in their stockings again. The cups and the cakes and the candy were almost too much. They were too happy to speak. But Ma asked if they were sure the stockings were empty.

Then they put their arms down inside them, to make sure. And in the very toe of each stocking was a shining bright, new penny!

They had never even thought of such a thing as having a penny. Think of having a whole penny for your very own. Think of having a cup and a cake and a stick of candy *and* a penny.

There had never been such a Christmas.

LAURA INGALLS WILDER

Monday, Dec. 27, 1943
Dear Kitty,

On Friday evening for the first time in my life I
received something for Christmas. Koophius and
the Kraler girls had prepared a lovely surprise again.
Miep had made a lovely Christmas cake, on which
was written "Peace 1944." Elli had provided a
pound of sweet biscuits of pre-war quality. For
Peter, Margot, and me a bottle of Yoghourt, and a
bottle of beer for each of the grownups. Everything
was so nicely done up, and there were pictures stuck
on the different parcels. Otherwise Christmas
passed by quickly for us.

Yours,
Anne

Anne Frank

. . . I can never remember whether it snowed
for six days and six nights when I was twelve or
whether it snowed for twelve days and twelve nights
when I was six; or whether the ice broke and the
skating grocer vanished like a snow man through a
white trap-door on that same Christmas Day that
the minced pies finished Uncle Arnold and we
tobogganed down the seaward hill, all the
afternoon, on the best tea-tray, and Mrs. Griffiths
complained, and we threw a snowball at her niece,
and my hands burned so, with the heat and the
cold, when I held them in front of the fire, that I
cried for twenty minutes and then had some jelly.

Dylan Thomas

God rest ye merry, Innocents,
Let nothing you dismay,
Let nothing wound an eager heart
Upon this Christmas day.

OGDEN NASH

Jo was the first to wake in the grey dawn of
Christmas morning. No stockings hung at the
fireplace, and for a moment she felt as much
disappointed as she did long ago, when her little
sock fell down because it was so crammed with
goodies. Then she remembered her mother's
promise, and, slipping her hand under her pillow,
drew out a little crimson-covered book. She knew it
very well, for it was that beautiful old story of the
best life ever lived, and Jo felt that it was a true
guidebook for any pilgrim going the long journey.
She woke Meg with a "merry Christmas," and bade
her see what was under her pillow. A green-covered
book appeared, with the same picture inside, and a
few words written by their mother, which made
their one present very precious in their own eyes.
Presently, Beth and Amy woke, to rummage and
find their little books also—one dove-colored, the
other blue; and all sat looking at and talking about
them, while the east grew rosy with the coming day.

LOUISA MAY ALCOTT

The more money you spend on a toy, the
more likely the kids will be to play with the box it
came in.

GEORGE PERRET

She had a splendid Christmas. She went to bed early, so as to let Santa Claus have a chance at the stockings, and in the morning she was up the first of anybody and went and felt them, and found hers all lumpy with packages of candy, and oranges and grapes, and pocket-books and rubber balls and all kinds of small presents, and her brother's with nothing but tongs in them, and her young lady sister's with a new silk umbrella, and her papa's and her mamma's with potatoes and pieces of coal wrapped up in tissue paper, just as they always had every Christmas. Then she waited around till the rest of the family were up, and she was the first to burst into the library, when the doors were opened, and look at the large presents laid out on the library table—books, and portfolios, and boxes of stationery, and breast pins, and dolls, and little stoves, and dozens of handkerchiefs, and ink stands, and skates, and snow-shovels, and photograph frames, and little easels, and boxes of watercolors, and Turkish paste, and nougat, and candied cherries, and dolls' houses, and waterproofs—and the big Christmas-tree, lighted and standing in a waste-basket in the middle.

She had a splendid Christmas all day. . . .

WILLIAM DEAN HOWELLS

My grandmother waited for a fortnight or longer after Christmas before she proffered her gifts to family, neighbors and friends. By early January, she concluded, expectation would have vanished and satiety be forgotten; in other words, the first fine careless rapture of sudden surprise and pleasure might again be abroad in the world. She invariably chose a dull or dark day upon which to deliver her presents. . . .

I remember how once as children we met her thus burdened on our way home from school.

"You're rather late for Christmas, Grandmother," we ventured together.

"So, my dears, were the Three Wise Men!" she said.

MARY ELLEN CHASE

Toyland, Toyland
Little girl and boy-land
While you dwell within it
You are ever happy then.

GLEN MAC DONOUGH

VI

A DAY OF JOY AND FEASTING

A day of joy and feasting
Of happiness and mirth;
And every year it cometh here
To gladden all the earth.

wish you a merry Christmas
And a Happy New Year;
A pocket full of money
And a cellar full of beer,
And a great fat pig
To last you all the year.

OLD ENGLISH SONG

All you that to feasting and mirth are inclined,
Come, here is good news for to pleasure your mind,
Old Christmas is come for to keep open house,
He scorns to be guilty of starving a mouse:
Then come, boys, and welcome for diet the chief,
Plum-pudding, goose, capon, minced pies and roast
   beef.

TRADITIONAL

Come, bring with a noise,
   My merry, merry boys
The Christmas log to the firing:
   While my good dame, she
   Bids you all be free;
And drink to your heart's desiring.

ROBERT HERRICK

The Christmas family party that we mean, is not a mere assembling of relations, got up at a week or two's notice, originating this year, having no family precedent in the last, and not likely to be repeated in the next. It is an annual gathering of all the accessible members of the family, young or old, rich or poor; and all the children look forward to it, for two months beforehand, in a fever of anticipation. Formerly, it was held at grandpapa's; but grandpapa getting old, and grandmamma getting old too, and rather infirm, they have given up housekeeping, and domesticated themselves with uncle George, so the party always takes place at uncle George's house, but grandmamma sends in most of the good things, and grandpapa always *will* toddle down, all the way to Newgate-market, to buy the turkey, which he engages a porter to bring home behind him in triumph, always insisting on the man's being rewarded with a glass of spirits, over and above his hire, to drink "a merry Christmas and a happy New Year. . . ." As to grandmamma, she is very secret and mysterious for two or three days beforehand, but not sufficiently so to prevent rumours getting afloat that she has purchased a beautiful new cap with pink ribbons for each of the servants, together with sundry books, and penknives and pencil cases, for the younger branches; to say nothing of divers secret additions to the order originally given by aunt George at the pastrycook's, such as another dozen of mince-pies for the dinner, and a large plum-cake for the children.

CHARLES DICKENS

Christmas when I was growing up was always the same—same people, same food, same place. The whole family gathered at my grandparents' home. There was never anything out of the ordinary from year to year, but that's why I looked forward to the holidays so much—Christmas was the one thing that didn't change in a changing world. Even though I was young, I was aware of a sense of security that came from knowing that certain things you treasure will always be the same.

SABRINA LE BEAUF

The Grocers'! oh the Grocers'! Nearly closed, with perhaps two shutters down; but through those gaps such glimpses! It was not alone that the scales descending on the counter made a merry sound, or that the twine and roller parted company so briskly, or that the cannisters were rattled up and down like juggling tricks, or even that the blended scents of tea and coffee were so grateful to the nose, or even that the raisins were so plentiful and rare, the almonds so extremely white, the sticks of cinnamon so long and straight, the other spices so delicious, the candied fruits so caked and spotted with molten sugar as to make the coldest lookers-on feel faint. . . .

CHARLES DICKENS

Now all our neighbours' chimneys smoke,
And Christmas blocks are burning;
The ovens they with baked meats choke,
And all their spits are turning.
    Without the door let sorrow lie,
    And if for cold it hap to die,
    We'll bury 't in a Christmas pie,
And everymore be merry.

GEORGE WITHER

Christmas has come; let every man
Eat, drink, be merry all he can.
Ale's my best mark, but if port wine
Or whiskey's yours—let it be mine;
No matter what lies in the bowls,
We'll make it rich with our own souls.

WILLIAM HENRY DAVIES

God rest you merry gentlemen,
Let nothing you dismay,
Remember Christ our Saviour
Was born on Christmas Day,
To save poor souls from Satan's power
Which had long time gone astray;
And it's tidings of comfort and joy,
Comfort and joy.

OLD ENGLISH CAROL

Fail not to call to mind, in the course of the
twenty-fifth of this month, that the Divinest Heart
that ever walked the earth was born on that day;
and then smile and enjoy yourselves for the rest of
it; for mirth is also of Heaven's making.

LEIGH HUNT

At Christmas be merry and thank God of all,
And feast thy poor neighbors, the great and the
    small.
Yea, all the year long have an eye to the poor,
And God shall send luck to keep open thy door.

THOMAS TUSSER

The coach was crowded, both inside and out,
with passengers, who, by their talk, seemed
principally bound to the mansions of relations or
friends, to eat Christmas dinner. It was loaded with
hampers of game, and baskets and boxes of
delicacies, and hares hung dangling from their long
ears about the coachman's box—presents from
distant friends for the impending feast.

WASHINGTON IRVING

There is no Christmas like a home Christmas
with your Dad and Mother, Sis and brother there.
With their hearts humming at your home-coming,
and that merry yuletide spirit in the air.

CARL SIGMAN

125

. . . the great fire was banked high and red in the grate and the green ivy and red holly made you feel so happy and when dinner was ended the big plum pudding would be carried in, studded with peeled almonds and sprigs of holly, with bluish fire running around it and a little green flag flying from the top.

James Joyce

. . . But now the plates being changed by Miss Belinda, Mrs. Cratchit left the room alone—too nervous to bear witnesses—to take the pudding up, and bring it in.

Suppose it should not be done enough! Suppose it should break in turning out! Suppose somebody should have got over the wall of the backyard, and stolen it, while they were merry with the goose—a supposition at which the two young Cratchits became livid! All sorts of horrors were supposed.

Hallo! A great deal of steam! The pudding was out of copper. A smell like a washday. That was the cloth. A smell like an eating-house and a pastry cook's next door to each other, with a laundress's next door to that. That was the pudding! In half a minute, Mrs. Cratchit entered—flushed but smiling proudly—with the pudding, like a speckled canon ball, so hard and firm, blazing in half of half a quartern of ignited brandy, and bedight with Christmas holly stuck into the top.

Oh, what a wonderful pudding!

Charles Dickens

There never was such a goose. Bob said he
didn't believe there ever was such a goose cooked.
Its tenderness and flavour, size and cheapness, were
the themes of universal admiration. Eked out by
apple sauce and mashed potatoes, it was a sufficient
dinner for the whole family; indeed, as Mrs.
Cratchit said with great delight (surveying one
small atom of a bone upon the dish) they hadn't ate
it all at last!

CHARLES DICKENS

When the cloth was removed, the butler
brought in a huge silver vessel of rare and curious
workmanship, which he placed before the squire. Its
appearance was hailed with acclamation, being the
Wassail bowl, so reknowned in Christmas festivity.
The contents had been prepared by the squire
himself, being a beverage on the skillful mixture of
which he particularly prided himself; alleging it was
too abstruse and complex for the comprehension of
an ordinary servant. It was a potation, indeed, that
might well make the heart of a toper leap within
him; consisting of the richest and raciest wines,
highly spiced and sweetened, with roasted apples
bobbing about the surface.

WASHINGTON IRVING

25 Christmas Day. Lay pretty long in bed, and then rose, leaving my wife desirous to sleep, having sat up till four this morning seeing her mayds make mince pies. I to Church, where our parson Mills made a good sermon. Then home, and dined on some good ribs of beef roasted and mince pies; only my wife, brother, and Barker, and plenty of good wine of my owne; and thanks to God Almighty for the goodness of my condition at this day.

SAMUEL PEPYS
from his diary for 1666,
the year of the Great
London Fire.

Baking gingerbread perfumes a house like nothing else. It is good eaten warm or cool, iced or plain. And it improves with age, should you be lucky enough or restrained enough to keep it around for any length of time.

. . . Gingerbread is definitely food for a cold climate, its warm, deep taste the perfect thing on a winter afternoon. Ginger warms up your insides (and is believed by many to purify the blood). Gingerbread is ideal for a child's tea; it is amazing how very young children love spicy things. When you serve it to adults, once they have stopped giving you a funny look, they often say, "Gingerbread! I haven't had that in years."

LAURIE COLWIN

. . . in Ravloe village the bells rang merrily,
and the Church was fuller than all through the rest
of the year, with red faces among the abundant
dark-green boughs—faces prepared for a longer
service than usual by an arduous breakfast of toast
and ale. The green boughs, the hymn and anthem
never heard but at Christmas . . . brought the
vague exhulting sense, for which grown men could
as little have found words as the children, that
something great and mysterious had been done for
them in heaven above and in earth below, which
they were appropriating by their presence. And then
the red faces made their way through the black
biting frost to their own houses, feeling themselves
free for the rest of the day to eat, drink and be
merry, and using that Christmas freedom without
diffidence.

GEORGE ELIOT

Three hours and fifteen minutes later we were
off the stage and on our way back to Elmendorf
and Christmas dinner.

The flight from King Salmon was very festive.
Everbody was in a mellow mood. Coming into
Elmendorf Field, I was up in the cockpit talking on
the radio to the tower, trading a few jokes. I asked
the tower man, "When are you going to clear us for
landing—we're late for Christmas dinner." He
replied, "You can land as soon as we get this big fat
red-faced guy with the reindeer out of the flight
pattern."

BOB HOPE

ittle Jack Horner
Sat in a corner
Eating a Christmas pie;
He put in his thumb
And pulled out a plum
And said, "What a good boy am I."

NURSERY RHYME

But of all the preparations, the animal cookies
are the most fondly remembered.

Mama made them from a recipe given her by
Papa's mother, using the cookie cutters which had
also been hers. A sugar cookie dough it was, rolled
to paper thinness and cut into the shapes of dogs
and horses and camels and rabbits and chickens and
reindeer. There were also stars and Christmas trees,
but we liked the animal ones best, going back as
they did to the legend of that first Christmas when
the animals were said to have knelt in worship
before the baby, Jesus.

Once the cookies were out of the oven, the
work had barely started. They must then be iced
with white frosting and decorated. I have spent
hours setting raisin eyes in the heads of those
cookies, and still more time swirling colored icing in
loops on trees and stars. Then, red and green sugar
must be sprinkled over the entire surface. When
they were finally finished, the cookies were almost
(but not quite) too beautiful to eat.

LOULA GRACE ERDMAN

As the great day neared, the pace of preparation for the Christmas feast accelerated. The heavy damask tablecloth woven with a design of shamrocks, a wedding present to Grandmother from relatives in Ireland, was taken from its storage place. Along with the vast monogrammed matching napkins, it was kept wrapped in blue tissue paper (to preserve its whiteness) and produced only on the most festive of occasions. Then there were the cut-glass bowls and dishes and stemware, also from Ireland. All were washed in steaming, soapy ammoniated water until they gleamed like ice crystals under a winter sun. And out came the odd silver serving pieces, such as the dressing spoon with a twelve-inch handle, all to be burnished in turn into brilliance.

IRENE CORBALLY KUHN

Take a pheasant, a hare, a capon, two partridges and two pigeons. Chop them up, take out as many bones as you can, and add the livers and hearts, two kidneys from a sheep, force meat made into balls with eggs, pickled mushrooms, salt, pepper, spice, and vinegar. Boil the bones to make a good broth. Put the meat into a crust of good paste made craftily into the likeness of a bird's body. Pour in the liquor, close it up and bake it well. And so serve it forth with the head of one of the birds at one end and a great tail at the other, and divers of his long feathers set all about him.

A late 14th-century recipe for mince pie.

They served up salmon, venison and wild boars
By hundreds and by dozens and by scores
Hogsheads of honey, kilderkins of mustard,
Muttons and fatted beeves and bacon swine;
Herons and bitterns, peacocks, swan and bustard,
Teal, mallard, pigeons, widgeons, and in fine
Plum puddings, pancakes, apple pies and custard,
And there withal they drank good gascon wine,
With mead and ale and cider of our own
For porter, punch and negus were not known.

WHISTLECRAFT (JOHN H. FRERE)
from a description of King Arthur's
Christmas feast with the Knights
of the Round Table.

All the meat was from the home place, too.
Turkey, of course, and most useful of all, the
goose—the very one which had chased me the
summer before, hissing and darting out its bill at
the end of its curving neck like a feathered snake.
Here was the universal bird of an older Christmas:
its down was plucked, washed, and hung in bags in
the barn to be put into pillows; its awkward body
was roasted until the skin was crisp as fine paper;
and the grease from its carcass was melted down, a
little camphor added, and rubbed on the chests of
coughing children. We ate, slept on, and wore that
goose.

PAUL ENGLE

Christmas itself may be called into question
If carried so far it creates indigestion.

ANONYMOUS

The fact is that at every peal from this little
devil of a bell, the chaplain forgets his Mass and
allows his mind to wander to the Christmas supper.
He evokes visions of busy kitchens, with ovens
glowing like furnaces, warm vapors rising from
under tin lids, and through these vapors, two
superb turkeys, stuffed, crammed, mottled with
truffles. Or then again, he sees long files of little
pages carrying great dishes wrapped in their
tempting fumes, and with them he is about to enter
the dining hall. What ecstasy! Here stands the
immense table, laden and dazzling with peacocks
dressed in their feathers, pheasants spreading their
bronzed wings, ruby-colored decanters, pyramids of
luscious fruit amid the foliage. . . . This beatific
vision is so vivid that Dom Balaguère actually
fancies that the glorious dishes are being served
before him, on the very embroideries of the altar
cloths, and instead of saying *Dominus vobiscum,* he
catches himself saying the *Benedicite.*

ALPHONSE DAUDET
translated by
Antoinette Ogden.

There was stuffed Canada goose with the buffalo-berry jelly; ham boiled in a big kettle in the lean-to; watercress salad; chow-chow and pickles; dried green beans cooked with bacon, turnips, mashed potatoes and gravy, with coffee from the start to the pie, pumpkin and gooseberry. . . .

There were people at the table for hours. The later uninvited guests got sausage and sauerkraut, squash, potatoes, and fresh bread, with canned plums and cookies for dessert. Still later there was a big roaster full of beans and side meat brought in by a lady homesteader, and some mince pies made with wild plums to lend tartness instead of apples, which cost money.

MARI SANDOZ

Of course, there will be an apple pudding at such a season. Steamed in a lard bucket and cut open with a string. A sauce of oranges and lemons to make an ocean around each steaming volcano of suet and russet apples as it falls crumbling from the loop of twine. It will have to be steamed in the boiler, if your Christmas is to be the size of ours, and cooked in a ten-pound lard pail. Better use a cod line instead of the twine of other holidays, to parcel it out to members of the clan.

ROBERT P. TRISTRAM COFFIN

assail

1.8 litres (3 pints) ale
15 gr. (½ ounce) ground ginger
15 gr. (½ ounce) ground nutmeg
250 gr. (8 ounces) dark brown sugar

½ bottle sherry or Madeira
2 lemons
3 lumps sugar
12 crab apples or 6 small red apples

Place 2½ cups of the ale in a saucepan, add the
ginger, nutmeg, and the brown sugar, and bring to
the boil. Rub the lumps of sugar on the outside of
one of the lemons, to remove all the zest. Thinly
slice the other lemon. Add the sugar lumps, the
sherry or Madeira, and the rest of the ale to the
saucepan, and make it very hot, but do not boil.
Place the lemon slices in a large bowl, and pour the
hot liquid over them. Add the sizzling roasted
apples. To roast the apples: Slit the skin for easier
cooking, and bake the apples in a moderate oven
until their texture looks soft and mashable. During
cooking, baste with a little ale if they appear to be
becoming too dry.

BRENDA MARSHALL
from The Charles Dickens
Cookbook.

The brown bowle,
The merry brown bowle,
As it goes round about-a,
    Fill
    Still,
Let the world say what it will,
And drink your fill all out-a.

The deep canne,
The merry deep canne,
As thou dost freely quaff-a
    Sing
    Fling,
Be merry as a king,
And sound a lusty laugh-a.

WASSAIL SONG

Everywhere,
everywhere,
Christmas tonight!
Christmas in
lands of the
fir-trees and pine,
Christmas in
lands of the
palm-tree and vine
Christmas where
snow peaks stand
solemn and white . . .
Christmas where
peace, like a dove
in its flight
Broods o'er
brave men in the
thick of the fight;
Everywhere,
everywhere,
Christmas tonight.

PHILLIPS BROOKS

"MERRY CHRISTMAS
TO ALL AND TO ALL A
GOOD NIGHT"

SANTA CLAUS